Growing
Organic Berries

Exactly How To Grow, Maintain & Preserve Every Type Of Berry To Support A Healthy Lifestyle

Adam Holmes

Copyright © 2014 Adam Holmes
ClydeBank Publishing
All rights reserved.

ISBN-13 : 978-1500816100

CONTENTS

INTRODUCTION

If you're anything like me, you like being healthy and y
like keeping your hard earned money. I hate paying for
overpriced fruit at the grocery store, farmers market and
organic shops. What I hate even more than the absurd
is the subpar quality and toxic ingredients.

Listen, if you are a health conscious individual you
are already familiar with the numerous scientific studie
that prove the definitive health benefits of organic food
you aren't you should educate yourself and understan
repercussions of ingesting pesticides and GMOs. This
is about growing organic berries, something you can d
home to take the middleman out of the equation and
quality fresh fruit right into your house, all year round
you choose not to purchase this book, if you choose
to grow your own organic berries, please, at the very
commit to a healthier lifestyle that substitutes proces
engineered, contaminated products for their organic

counterparts. Know what you are putting in your body, simple enough.

If you are so brave as to take the next step and start your own organic fruit and vegtable production, then berries are a great starting point. Not only are they simple to grow, they are able to be easily persevered for months to come so you can enjoy them all year round. This book will teach you everything you need to know to go from someone who can only name 3 berries, to an individual that can provide his family, friends and neighbors (for charity, or profit) with enough organic berries for years to come.

Sounds simple enough, right. It is. Follow me on journey to a world you wish you were found earlier. I romise you'll be sorry you didn't start earlier.

ONE

Starting With The Basics

Berries can make a great addition to your garden whether you decide to plant them indoors or outdoors. They are known to have wonderful health benefits and have been used in medicinal purposes since ancient times. They also have a variety of culinary uses, and you just have to plant them alongside your other crops in your kitchen garden. From salads, desserts, beverages, to wines - berries will make your menu at home delectably colorful and vibrant.

THE BENEFITS OF GROWING BERRIES

1. Growing Your Own Superfoods

Blackberries, blueberries, raspberries, and strawberries are considered to be superfoods that are very valuable to the market nowadays. They are pack with nutrients that keep the body strong and healthy for a long time. They also contain antioxidants and phytochemicals that prevent, and at times reverse, the effects of aging. They are also helpful in keeping arthritis, cardiovascular diseases, certain types of cancer, and high blood pressure at bay.

2. Keep Your Shelves Stocked With Healthy Brain Food

Berries such as blueberries are very potent against mental illnesses such as dementia and Alzheimer's. Berries are also good for diabetics since it is low on the glycemic index. For people watching their weight, berries are great alternatives to junk food and fast food. Plus, they are sweet and delicious!

3. Provide Your Family With Healthier Dishes

There's a plethora of delicious berry recipes out there for you to try out once you have harvested your precious berries from the garden. From beverages to jams, from pies to wines, berries are great whether you eat them fresh or cooked.

4. Create A Beautiful & Productive Space In Your Home

Whether you have an ample outdoor area to grow berries or somewhat little on space, it is very much possible to grow berries outside or inside your home. Berries do not only produce healthy fruits, but they also make great ornamentals in your abode. Nature has indeed made it possible to blend beauty with purpose in tiny little packages - which are berries of course.

This Book will be your handy partner in growing berries indoors and outdoors. First off, you will be introduced to the different types of berries out there, wherein some are edible and some are poisonous. Next up, there will be step-by-step guides in growing different types of berries. You will also know how to effectively plant and grow berries in containers so that you can easily move them outside or inside your home. There are also helpful worksheets at the near end of this eBook to help you plan, schedule, and grow your own garden of berries. To further help you on your quest for quality seeds and resources, there is a chapter on highly recommended sites online for your own perusal.

I will take you by the hand and lead you every step of the way to successfully grow your own berries - the superfoods of this day and age. The health benefits of berries cannot be overemphasized. Growing them in your own backyard, or even in front of a window sill, will do wonders to your health and environment.

TWO

Berry Varieties

The scientific definition of berries is that they are fleshy fruits produced from a single ovary of a plant. A berry commonly develops as a fleshy fruit when the entire ovary wall of plant ripens into a pericarp, which is the edible tissue around the seeds.

There are more than five thousand species of berries in the world, each with its own characteristics and benefits. Some are useful to humans while some cannot be eaten. Most berries are round but come in a myriad of colors. Each one tastes differently and may have seeds inside or not. To help you decide which type of berry to procure and plant in your own garden, here's a list with information about berries for your own perusal.

BOTANICAL BERRIES

Botanical berries are considered to be the ones that show characteristics according to the scientific definition of a berry. They are fruits that have seeds and pulp produced from a single ovary of a plant. Botanical berries develop from the superior ovary.

Avocado - Avocados are scientifically classified as berries, specifically one-seeded berries. They are grown in Mediterranean and tropical regions around the world and are highly valuable in the market.

Barberry - Barberry plants are evergreen and deciduous shrubs that grow from one to five meters tall and have thorny shoots. Its fruit extracts are known to have antihistamine and anti-allergy properties. It is also good for the immune system of the body. In India, it is used to treat diarrhea, fever, upset stomach, and improve appetite.

Bearberry - Bearberries are brown or reddish in color. It also has several medicinal uses such as in the treatment of kidney stones, nephritis, and lowering uric acid content in the body.

Coffee Berries - Coffee berries are considered to be one of the most valuable crops in the world that is widely traded as a commodity. This black gold is exported by several countries and has moved many economies.

Crowberry - Crowberries are dry and black color, which have a similar appearance and taste to blueberries. They are used as natural food coloring and as an ingredient in jellies and pies.

Currant - Black currant is high in Vitamin C, Vitamin B5, potassium, phosphorous, and iron. It is also used in ice creams, jams, pies, and tarts. Red currants, on the other hand, are also high in Vitamin C, potassium, iron, and fiber. They are generally used in salads, tarts, and jams.

Elderberry - Elderberries are small, usually black or blue, and grow in clusters. They are rich in anthocyanins and antioxidants. The berries are mainly used in cake mix, muffins, jams, and syrups.

Goji Berries - Goji berries are usually found dried and shriveled up and are red in color. The berries are rich in minerals, amino acids, vitamins, carbohydrates, proteins, fiber, and so much more. They are usually cooked before being consumed. The berries are also used in wines, rice congee, juices, and herbal teas.

Grapes - Grapes are rich in Vitamin A, Vitamin, C, Vitamin B6, calcium, folic acid, magnesium, and potassium. Besides being generally used in wines, they also make great homemade jellies.

Gooseberry - Gooseberry bushes grow to a height of up to three meters with thick and sharp spines. It grows well in humid summers and winter chill in cool regions. The color of its fruit may be green, yellow, white, or may come in shades of red, pink, purple, and black. It is rich in carbohydrates, fiber, minerals, protein, and vitamins. It also contains a potent polyphenol called Gallic acid.

Honeysuckle - The berries are generally red, blue, or black in color with a spherical and elongated shape and with several seeds in it. Some species are edible and grown in home gardens, while some are mildly poisonous.

Indian Gooseberry - Indian gooseberries, also known as Amla or Amalika, are indigenous in India. The berries grow on small to medium sized trees and have a variety of health benefits. They are generally sour in taste and are rich in fiber. It has many uses in Ayurvedic medicine.

Lingonberry or Cowberry - Lingonberries are generally red in color. They are rich in Vitamin C, Vitamin B, and provitamin-A. It has a variety of uses such as in making compotes, sauces, jams, juices, and syrups.

Nannyberry - Nannyberries can grow into a large shrub or small tree. It is indigenous in Southern Canada and North Eastern United States. Several parts of the plant including the berries, seeds, leaves, and bark are used to treat a variety of conditions such as digestive, menstrual, and respiratory problems. It can also relieve anxiety and pain.

Oregon-grape - These berries are purple or blue in color and look like grapes. They also look like they are covered with a powdery substance. The berries also have antibacterial and anti-inflammatory properties.

Persimmon - Persimmons are scientifically classified as berries. They are indigenous in Asia and the Middle East, and they are also grown in the Southern United States. They are round in shape, mealy in texture, and tart in taste.

Tomato - A common kitchen ingredient, tomatoes are scientifically classified as berries. Tomatoes have several culinary uses and have various health benefits.

MODIFIED BERRIES

Modified berries are those fruits that have a thick rind and juicy interior. The difference of modified berries from botanical berries is that the former develops from the inferior ovary of the plant while the latter develops from the superior ovary.

Bilberry - Bilberries are low-growing shrubs that are also known as blaeberry, myrtle blueberry, whinberry, or whortleberry. They are usually eaten fresh, but they are also turned into juices, jams, and pies. Bilberries are one of the healthiest berries around as they have tannins that have anti-inflammatory and astringent properties, plus flavonoids which are antioxidants. They also offer relief for hemorrhoids, capillary weakness, and venous insufficiency.

Blueberry - Blueberries are seen growing in the wild and also cultivated in farms. The fruit is round, blue, and with flared crowns in one end. The fruit is seen as white at first, then it turns into reddish purple up until it becomes blue when it ripens. Besides being used in jams, jellies, and pies, it has a number of health benefits. It has a large amount of phytonutrients that help the body's resistance towards diseases. It also improves antioxidant activity, which protects the body from oxidative stress and other cardiovascular diseases.

Cranberry - Cranberries are at first white and then turn red when they ripen. The berries contain Vitamin C, fiber, manganese, and minerals. They are highly used in sauces, juices, and wines. Many have also discovered the wonderful health benefits of cranberry, especially in weight management.

Farkleberry - Also known as Sparkleberry, these berries are related to blueberries and is indigenous in the Midwest. They don't have a specific taste, yet animals love to eat them.

Huckleberry - Huckleberries are sweet and rich in antioxidants. It is usually used in supplements to improve blood flow to the heart, keep blood vessels strong, and lessen the risk of atherosclerosis. The leaves of Huckleberry is also used in tea.

DRUPES

There are various fruits that are commonly referred to as berries but do not fall into the scientific definition of a berry. One such classification are drupes which are fleshy fruits that develop from a hard endocarp layer surrounding a single-seeded ovary.

Acai Berry - Acai berries are small and round with a black color. The fruit is Brazil's biggest cash crop due to its various health benefits and title as 'superfood'. The fruit is rich in antioxidants, vitamins, minerals, and fiber. It is mainly used in smoothies, juices, and many other beverages.

Barbados Cherry - This type of berry grows in small shrubs or trees which are indigenous in Central to South America and the Caribbean. It is rich in Vitamin C, Vitamin A, Vitamin B1, B2, B3, carotenoids, and bioflavonoids. It also has antioxidant properties. It is highly edible and used in juices and liquor. The plant is also turned into bonsai and other ornamental purposes.

Bayberry - The wax coating found in these berries are traditionally used in making candles. It has also been used in fresh, canned, and dried goods. It is also used in juice and alcoholic beverages as well as to spice beer and snaps.

Buffaloberry - Buffaloberries are indigenous in many parts of Northern America. The berries are large and red with a relatively bitter taste. It has been used in dyes, food, and medicine. They can be eaten fresh or dried. They are also used in many baked goods.

Cherries - Cherries are rich in antioxidants, which are known to help promote healthy cells and tissues in the body. They are also high in anthocyanins and bioflavonoids, which can reduce muscle and joint discomfort. They also contain melatonin, which promotes youthful complexion and healthy sleep patterns.

Chokecherry - Chokecherries are indigenous in many parts of the West and can be easily cultivated in gardens. They are also rich in antioxidants, which promotes optimum health. They also make great syrups and jams.

Indian Plum - Indian plums, or also known as osoberries, have a darkish blue or plum color and were used as medicine by the Native Americans.

Sea-Buckthorn Berry - These berries are orange, soft, and juicy. The berries are high in Vitamin C, Vitamin E, amino acids, carotenoids, and dietary minerals. They are also rich in oil and has many nutritional benefits. They have a variety of uses such as in the making of jams, liquors, lotions, and pies.

POMES

Pomes are classified as having a structure that separates

the seeds from the ovary tissue. There are smaller pomes that are sometimes referred to as berries.

Chokeberries - These berries are small in size and are very bitter in taste. It is rich in antioxidants and Vitamin C. It is used in coloring, flavoring, jams, juices, wines, and many others purposes.

Hawberries - Hawberries are usually bright red in color and look like crabapple fruits. They are used to make hawflakes, alcoholic beverages, jams, juices, jellies, and many other drinks. They can also be eaten fresh or cooked. Many of its species are also used in ornamental purposes.

Juneberries or Saskatoon Berries - Juneberries are red at first and then turn bluish black when they ripen. They are also similar in size to blackberries. The berries can be made into great cobblers, muffins, and jams.

Serviceberries - These berries classified as pomes are red to purple in color and are very sweet in taste. It is used in desserts such as pies and jams.

Wild Rose or Rosehips - These berries are red in color and oval in shape. They are the fruits of certain rose plant species. They are also high in Vitamin C.

AGGREGATE FRUITS

Aggregate fruits contain seeds from different ovaries of a single flower from a plant.

Blackberry - Blackberries grow extensively and up to a height of three meters. They grow best in woods and hillsides and they can spread widely, even in poor soil conditions. The fruits of Blackberry are used in wine, jams, and various desserts.

Boysenberry - Boysenberry is a cross between blackberries, loganberries, and raspberries. The color of its fruit is deep maroon and it is generally large, glossy, and juicy. They are mainly used in pies and as decoration in tarts and cheesecakes.

Dewberry - These are wild berries that grow on vines and are indigenous in the Pacific Northwest. They have a slightly bitter taste, but they can still be eaten fresh. They are also used in baked goods and jams.

Marionberry - Marionberries are an indigenous blackberry that is a cross between Ollaliberry and Chehalem cultivars. It is darker than blackberries and glossy in appearance. It is used in many desserts such as ice creams, jellies, and pies.

Raspberry - Raspberries are similar to blackberries, but they have a different size and color. It also spreads widely and grows in fields and forests. They have hollow cores and are the most delicate of all berries. It is recommended that you use raspberries quickly since they don't last very long.

Cloudberry - Cloudberries are a dwarf species of raspberry. It is a pale red fruit which grows to a height of twenty-five meters and turns into an amber color during fall season. Cloudberries are rich in Vitamin C and is known as a supplement for scurvy and urinary tract infections. It is also used as an ice cream topping in Sweden and as a flavoring in special beers in Canada.

Wineberry - Another type of raspberry, Wineberry or Japanese Wineberry comes in red or orange colors and has a diameter of one centimeter. They grow well in loamy and moist soil and bear fruit during summer or early fall. They are commonly used in pies or other sweet treats for their tart taste.

Tayberry - Tayberries are a cross between blackberries and raspberries. They are an extremely soft and fragrant variety. The fruits are also generally used in jams.

Loganberry - Loganberries are produced from the pollination of diploid red raspberry and an octaploid blackberry cultivar. It is characterized as ruby-red and has the shape of a blackberry. It turns purplish red when ripe and is very juicy and sweet. These berries are rich in Vitamin C, carbohydrates, fiber, calcium, iron, and potassium. They are mainly used in the preparation of juices.

Ollaliberry - Ollaliberries are a cross between

youngberries and loganberries. They also look the same as blackberries. They have a variety of uses such as in the making of ice cream toppings, yogurt, jams, and so much more.

Salmonberry - Also called Thimbleberries, Salmonberries are yellow to orange-red in color and has a sweet flavor. They are edible and used in candies, jams, jellies, and wines.

Youngberry - Youngberries are a cross between blackberries and dewberries. They are extensively grown in Australia, South Africa, and New Zealand.

MULTIPLE FRUITS

Multiple fruits are developed from a number of flowers in a plant that are merged together.

Mulberry - Mulberry trees grow fast up to a height of ten to fifteen meters. Its fruit is usually two to three centimeters long and is at first red which ripens to a dark purple. It is generally edible and is widely used in different regions. It is also highly preferred by birds.

ACCESSORY FRUITS

Accessory fruits are classified as edibles that are not developed by the ovary of the plant.

Strawberry - Strawberries are one of the most popular fruits that are being used for different purposes and eaten extensively all over the globe. They are rich in Vitamin C, folic acid, and manganese content. They have a variety of culinary uses such as in ice creams, jams, milk shakes, pies, and tarts.

Wintergreen - This type of plant grows as a vine and is indigenous in Canada and Northern United States. These berries are acerbic in taste which improves when frozen.

MODIFIED CONES

Juniper Berry - Juniper berries are actually false berries that are classified as modified cones. These berries are green in color at first and then turn into purplish black when they ripen. They have a variety of uses such as in the preparation of gin and the seasoning of cabbage, pork, and sauerkraut.

POISONOUS BERRIES

While some berries are healthy and have a number of uses, take note of the following berries which are actually toxic. Use a field guide or consult an expert when you encounter them in the wild.

Actea Pachypoda - Also known as doll's eyes, these are white berries that have a black dot on them. The plant produces white flowers and the berries are poisonous.

Baneberry - These are small berries that are white or red in color. They are known to be toxic.

Bittersweet - These berries are bright orange in color

and grow on vines. They taste extremely bitter and are toxic. They can only be used for ornamental purposes.

Daphne Berry - These berries grow on fragrant Daphne plants that have small and clustered pink or green flowers.

Elderberry - While the purple elderberries are safe to use in food and medicine, other parts of the plant such as the leaves, stems, and roots are poisonous. The bright red varieties of elderberry are also poisonous.

European Holly Berry - These are red berries that grow on holly plants which have white flowers.

Green Nightshade - These are poisonous green berries that grow on weedy plants.

Holly Berry - These are bright red berries that are toxic and grow on evergreen shrubs.

Ivy Berry - These are toxic berries found on ivy plants which are small and has a purple to black color.

Jerusalem Cherry - Jerusalem cherries look similar to cherry tomatoes. They are also poisonous so take caution when identifying.

Mistletoe Berry - These are toxic berries that have a small size, hard texture, and red color.

Pokeberry - Pokeberries look similar to blueberries, but all of its plant parts are toxic. They differ from blueberries in such a way that they lack the star at the base of its fruit and they have a glossy, purplish red sheen.

Privet Berry - Privet berries are small, toxic, black or purple berries that grow on evergreen or semi-evergreen shrubs or hedges.

Red Nightshade - These are poisonous red berries that grow on a plant which is considered a weed.

Yew Berry - These are toxic red berries which can be found on evergreen shrubs.

THREE

Growing Berries Indoors

If you are tight in outdoor space, you can actually grow berries indoors. Growing berries indoors will make your home lovely and vibrant. Plus, you will be having delicious and healthy berries to serve on the table. Here are just a few step-by-step guides on how to effectively grow your own berries at the comfort of your own home. The following guides are for common species of berries.

HOW TO GROW BLACKBERRIES INDOORS

Materials:

• Starter Blackberry Trees

• Big Container with a plate or saucer underneath

• Mesh

• Gravel

For the potting soil (use any of the following):

• Fertilizer Formula for Fruit Trees

• Equal parts peat, sand, and vermiculite

For added maintenance:

• Compost

• Bone Meal

• Mulch

• Water-soluble fertilizer

Steps:

1. Procure a starter blackberry plant from a highly recommended garden center or mail-order company. Choose an erect dwarf variety because this is suitable for growing in little indoor spaces. This type of variety is also sturdy and self-supporting, which is ideal since it is low maintenance.

2. The container that you will use to plant the blackberry should be big enough to hold a small tree, but lightweight enough so that you can easily move it around. You can use clay, ceramic, metal, plastic, or wood. You can also use a recycled barrel or wash tub.

3. Drill holes at the bottom of the container for drainage. Layer the bottom with mesh to ensure that the soil wouldn't be washed out when you water your plant. To further control drainage, spread a layer of gravel at the bottom.

4. Fill the container with a fertilizer formula specifically for fruit trees. You can also make your own potting soil by mixing equal parts peat, sand, and vermiculite.

5. Before transferring the blackberry seedling to the

container, trim away any unhealthy foliage and roots.

6. Plant the blackberry seedling at around five inches deep into the container. Fill the pot with the recommended soil mix and secure the soil evenly and firmly.

7. Add compost to the soil to allow your blackberry to grow in a healthy medium. You can also spread some bone meal around the blackberry plant and mix it with the soil, but just make sure that it is away from the blackberry cane. Top this off with mulch or bark chips as a layer of protection.

8. Place the blackberry tree where it can get as much sunlight as possible. Make sure that the plant is also protected from cold drafts and heating ducts since this can negatively affect the growth of your blackberry tree.

9. Water your blackberry only when the soil on top of the container is dry. Make sure that you don't over water your plant since this can negatively affect its growth. When winter comes, limit your watering since this is a time wherein the blackberry tree's growth slows down.

10. Fertilize your blackberry regularly or as recommended in the fertilizer packet. Water-soluble fertilizers work best for blackberry trees. To choose the best type of fertilizer, look for a product that has copper, iron, magnesium, manganese, nitrogen, phosphorous, potassium, and zinc in proper proportions. You will notice that the plant

has a nice shade of green on its foliage if you are fertilizing it properly.

11. The blackberry tree will produce a good harvest a year after you planted it indoors. Blackberry trees require a year before it matures and bears fruit. The berries from the tree should fall away easily from its branches and have a sweet taste.

12. After harvesting the berries, prune away the stems or branches that the berries came from. Leave the other stems to produce berries for the next harvesting season.

Additional Info: How to Grow Blackberries from Cuttings

You can actually grow more blackberries indoors from cuttings you procure from the mother plant. This will help you get more produce for the next harvesting season and provide you with more productive plants in your home garden.

Materials:

- Pruning shears
- Container
- Potting soil
- Small stones

Steps:

1. Start pruning in August or early September since

this is the most ideal time to start growing new seedlings. Make sure that the stems that you will prune are healthy and sturdy with no wounds or dead leaves. The stem should also be long enough that when it is bent, it touches the ground easily.

2. Dig a hole at least six inches deep that the top of the stem can reach into when it is bent over.

3. Bend the stem and stick it into the hole.

4. Bury the stem with soil. Surround the buried stem with stones to support it.

5. Wait for about two months so that the buried stem can grow roots.

6. Use your pruning shears to cut the stem at least 1 foot from the base of the rooted daughter vine to the mother blackberry vine.

7. Dig up the cutting with roots. Make sure that you do not damage the delicate root system of the young cutting.

8. Place the cutting into a container with rich potting soil. Keep it in a greenhouse or indoors until next spring.

9. Water the growing plant regularly, making sure that the soil is moist.

10. You can transplant the blackberry seedling into a more permanent container after the last frost towards the upcoming spring.

HOW TO GROW BLUEBERRIES INDOORS

Materials:

- Blueberry bushes
- Large containers
- Plastic trays
- Water-soluble fertilizer

For the soil mix:

- Potting soil
- Shredded peat moss
- Granular sulfur
- Shredded bark mulch

Steps:

1. Buy dwarf-type varieties of blueberry bushes. They are ideal for growing indoors. You can also buy several varieties so that they can cross pollinate for maximum production.

2. Get a large container that can contain at least five to ten gallons. You can use a recycled barrel or tub for this. Drill holes at the bottom for proper drainage.

3. Put plastic trays underneath the large container to catch excess water and to protect the floors from moisture damage.

4. Fill one-third of the container with equal amounts of potting soil and shredded peat moss.

5. Add two tablespoons of granular sulfur to the container. Mix the granular sulfur together with the soil, making sure that everything is incorporated well.

6. Put the root ball of the blueberry plant into the container. Push the soil around the roots gently. Then press the soil firmly to balance the plant.

7. Fill the container with more potting soil and peat moss, up until it reaches three inches below the rim.

8. Spread a one-inch layer of shredded bark mulch on top of the soil. Do make sure that it is substantially away from the trunk of the blueberry bush.

9. Place your blueberry plant near a window or on a balcony, patio, or terrace where it can get adequate sunlight all day long. Blueberries need at least six hours of sunshine in the morning, but need to be in a shade later in the day.

10. Fertilize your blueberry plant once a month. Water-soluble fertilizers work best with blueberries. You can sprinkle one tablespoon of fertilizer granules at the base of the plant, then water it to activate the compounds.

HOW TO GROW RASPBERRIES INDOORS

Materials:

• Tulameen or Tulameen tissue-cultured raspberry plug

• 5-gallon container

• Gravel

- Straw

- Thermometer

For the Soil Mix (equal parts):

- Peat

- Perlite

- Sand

- Vermiculite

Steps:

1. Start with two Tulameen tissue-cultured raspberry plugs so that you can use the other one to pollinate. This variety of raspberry grow excellently indoors, especially in greenhouses or inside your home.

2. During the month of May, give your plugs a fresh start by setting them up outside. Mix equal parts of peat, perlite, sand, and vermiculite in a five gallon container. Make sure that the container has holes at the bottom. If not, drill holes underneath that are at least one-half inch in diameter. Raspberries grow best when their roots are well-hydrated but not wet all the time.

3. Place the raspberry containers on top of a gravel patch. You can also buy some gravel, spread it around an area, and put the containers on top of them. This will ensure proper drainage for your plants.

4. Let your raspberry seedlings thrive during summer.

When winter comes, spread some straw around the containers to counteract the chill. This will allow the plants to be dormant, but not freeze and die against the weather.

5. Once the leaves of your raspberry plants drop and before the temperature drops to 10 or 15 degrees Fahrenheit, bring the plants inside your home. The weather would usually become this cold by mid-November to December.

6. Place your raspberry plants near a window. Check the temperature with a thermometer. Make sure that the plants dwell in an area with a temperature between 60 to 70 degrees.

7. The raspberry plants will produce flowers at around six weeks, and you might be seeing this at around mid-January.

8. To help pollinate your raspberries, use a paint brush or ear cotton bud to take the pollen from one flower to another. Since you have two raspberry plants, deliver the pollen from the flowers of one container to the flowers of the other container.

9. You can start harvesting raspberries after four weeks, which would usually happen during mid-February.

10. Allow your berries to become dormant so that it can be given some rest and grow productively again after several months. Cool weather will give it time to be dormant. You

can set it up again outside during May or place it in a cool space for it to become dormant.

11. Clip away all the canes of the raspberry plant, except four of its new ones. These canes will produce new crops next year.

HOW TO GROW STRAWBERRIES INDOORS

Strawberries have a shallow root system, so you can easily grow them in containers indoors. Place them along a sunny window, patio, balcony, or terrace. The best time to plant them is during spring, although you can still plant them any time during the year.

Materials:
- Strawberry seedling
- Container with saucer or dish
- Mesh cloth
- Potting Soil
- Watering spike or pipe

Steps:

1. Layer the holes of the plant container with a mesh cloth for proper drainage.

2. Fill the container with potting soil that has been moistened and added with fertilizer.

3. Place the strawberry seedling on the container and fill it with potting soil. Spread the roots over the soil and direct

it towards the center of the container.

4. The stems of the strawberry plant should stick out from the soil and grow upright.

5. Continue filling the container with potting soil up until it reaches two inches below the rim of the container.

6. Continue planting three or four more strawberry plants in the center of the container. Make sure that their spacing is even. Spread the roots evenly across the soil and cover them with at least one inch of soil.

7. Put a large saucer or dish underneath the container so that it can catch excess water. You can also buy strawberry plants in pots at garden centers and you just have to place a large enough dish or saucer beneath it.

8. Water the plant regularly during growing season. Make sure that the soil is moist. You can use a watering spike to water the lower portions of the container. You can also use a plastic pipe, drill a few holes on it, and fill the pipe with water. The water will drain out of the holes and into various levels within the container.

9. Make sure that your strawberry plants get sunlight all day long. They need at least six hours of sunshine to thrive well. Turn the container every two days so that all sides get enough sunshine. You may consider supplementing them with artificial light which you can buy at garden stores.

FOUR

Growing Berries Outdoors

Growing berries outside is one of the most fulfilling gardening activities you could ever do. They grow beautifully in a garden and provide a great environment around your vicinity. Berries also make a healthy addition to your daily meals, and your kids will love planting as well as eating them.

HOW TO GROW BLACKBERRIES OUTDOORS

Materials:

• Blackberry bush

• Compost

• Garden Shovel or Spade

Steps:

1. Prepare the patch of land that you will be growing your blackberries on. If the soil is clay or sandy, dig up the soil and mix it with lots of compost or manure. Your soil will be ready in about two months for planting.

You can also choose a place to plant where the canes of

the blueberry can climb over a wall, fence, arch, or pergola. Just make sure that the area gets adequate sunlight, but the roots of the blueberry plant must not be exposed to the sun.

2. During the fall season or mid-October, start planting your blackberry bush on your patch of land.

3. During early spring or May, sprinkle some compound fertilizer around your blueberry plants to improve their growth.

4. Regularly water the blueberry plant once the weather starts to get warmer. Keep the plant well-watered when the berries start to show color, as well as after harvesting them.

5. You will usually get a harvest from your blueberry plant around August. The berries will be white then turn to red and then bluish black. You will know that the berries are ready for picking when you can easily pick them up from the stalk. If they hold strong to the stalk, just leave them be for a few days and they will be ready for picking.

6. After harvesting, cut out the canes that have produced fruit to keep the blueberry plant healthy. Make sure to cut them out at soil level. The plant will grow new canes which will produce a new harvest next year. A rule of thumb is to keep the number of canes from six to eight per blueberry plant. Diseases may spread over new and excess canes, so cropping twice a year can avoid this. Do take note that you

need to tie in new canes when they start to grow.

HOW TO GROW BLUEBERRIES OUTDOORS

Materials:

• Blueberry plant

• Sulfur

• Compost

• Garden shovel or spade

• Pruning shears

Steps:

1. Blueberry plants love acidic soil, preferably with a pH of around 5.5. To make the soil around your area more acidic, add sulfur on it and mix it well with the soil to make it more suitable for the growth of blueberries.

2. Add compost as well to your soil. This will ensure that the soil is healthy enough for your blueberry plants to thrive.

3. Procure different varieties of blueberries that grow and produce at different periods all throughout the year. This will allow you to extend the harvesting times around July to September. You can also do with just one plant since blueberries are self-pollinating, and one plant can produce its own fruit.

4. Dig up a hole in the soil at around two and half feet wide and one foot deep. Put the blueberry plant's roots

inside the hole. Cover the roots with soil and press it firmly without compacting it.

5. Fertilize your blueberry plant during spring. Amend your soil with compost or fertilizers, but stay away from high-nitrogen types. You can also plant clover around your blueberries which will naturally add nitrogen to the soil.

6. Prune away rubbing and crossing branches from your blueberry plant as it grows. Thinning out the plant will help promote proper air circulation for it to thrive well.

7. Be patient as it takes time - around two years - for young branches to produce the berries you've been waiting for. When they start producing fruit, pick them up and don't let them fall to the ground.

8. Keep your blueberry plant clean by removing wilted leaves around it and other debris at its base.

9. To ensure that birds and other critters won't be feasting on your blueberries, spread a fine garden mesh or net around the plant to protect it.

HOW TO PLANT RASPBERRIES OUTDOORS

Materials:

- Raspberry canes
- Shovel
- Compost
- Mulch

- Stakes

- Thick wire

Steps:

1. Choose a location to plant where your raspberries can have full sunlight or partial shade. Make sure that it is also near a water source.

2. Raspberries love soil that has lots of moisture. Amend the soil with lots of compost or organic matter. Mix the soil and compost well before planting.

3. It is best to plant the raspberries during fall season. Plant your raspberry canes in a row.

4. Water your plants well before applying mulch.

5. After planting, cut the canes to the soil beneath them. They can grow a bit unmanageable during summer and they need to have strong support. Hammer in two stakes into the soil and attach thick wires to them at intervals of 24 inches. Tie the stems to them.

6. During the first year that the raspberry plant grows, take out any fruits that form to let the plant focus on growing its roots.

7. After each year of producing fruit, cut the canes that produced fruit to the ground. Tie new canes to the support you installed. These canes will produce fruit for the next harvesting season.

PRIMARY CONSIDERATIONS IN PLANTING STRAWBERRIES

1. Choose the type of strawberry you'd like to plant. There are basically two common types of strawberries: summer-producing strawberries and ever-bearing or perpetual strawberries. The summer-producing type will enable you to harvest a great supply of strawberries from early to mid-summer. You do have to plant them two months before so that they would produce fruit by the time summer comes.

The ever-bearing or perpetual strawberry variety will produce a substantial amount of fruit all throughout the year. They can be planted indoors or outdoors. They also grow productively for five or more years.

Day-neutral strawberry varieties are also similar to the perpetual strawberry variety, but will produce smaller amounts of strawberries all throughout the year. They are a great option if you want to eat strawberries fresh from the garden. If you want to make jams out of your strawberries, consider planting the Alpine variety of strawberries. This is a relatively small type of strawberry, but it is full of flavor.

2. Your local garden center may have the variety of strawberry you are looking for, but if they don't you can always check for mail order garden sites online and buy a

specific variety. Always ask which variety is perfect for your local climate.

Before buying always check the condition of your plants. The leaves of your strawberry plants should have a healthy shade of green without any spots or wilted parts. The roots should also be lightly colored and plentiful. You can also find disease-resistant varieties of strawberries to ensure that your plants can withstand most problems while growing. For more information on where to find disease-resistant varieties of plants, you can check out the Directory and Resources on Growing Berries on page 38.

Remember to buy the strawberry plants at the same period that you will be planting them in your garden. If you leave them to sit for too long in their temporary pots, they will be root-bound and become unhealthy for transplanting into the garden.

3. Decide the location of planting. Strawberries can thrive well indoors as well as outdoors - whether you choose to plant them in containers or garden beds. You do have to provide them with rich soil and fertilizer. If the weather gets cold, you have to put a cold frame around your strawberries or consider growing them in containers so that you can move them indoors.

Make sure that the location where you will plant your

strawberries get adequate sunlight all day long. Strawberries need direct sunlight without any shade. You may put them in a place with partial shade, but they won't be as productive as the ones receiving full sunlight. Make sure that the place you will be planting them gets minimal wind as well.

4. When planting, make sure that you do not cover the crown of a strawberry plant when planting it. However, the crown must only be sitting just above the ground that it is not too exposed.

5. The right time for planting strawberries will depend on what type of variety it is. Refer to the seed packet or seller of the strawberry on what month or season it should be planted.

For strawberries that produce large fruits, it is best to plant them during summer. Perpetual or ever-bearing varieties will grow well when planted during the fall season. Alpine varieties, on the other hand, are best to plant during the second to third months of spring.

6. Before planting strawberries on a garden bed, make sure that you remove any weeds or underlying roots that may hamper the growth of your plants. Afterwards, add a substantial amount of compost to the soil to provide a healthy foundation for your strawberries. Strawberries thrive well in soil rich in compost. You must do this as well

especially when the soil is heavy in sand or clay. If the soil is acidic, add three-fourths cup of dolomite for every square meter of complete plant food before you start planting. Mulch the soil after planting to protect the surface and to ensure that your strawberries remain clean.

7. Strawberries will continue being productive for five years or so until they need to be replaced. If you experience problems such as diseases or viruses destroying the strawberry plants, make sure to replace the strawberry stock every two years. You might want to consider buying new and disease-resistant varieties as well.

HOW TO PLANT STRAWBERRIES OUTDOORS

Materials:

• Strawberry Plant

• Bucket of Water

• Water-soluble fertilizer

Optional:

• Strawberry net or fine garden mesh

Steps:

1. Carefully take out the strawberry from its store-bought container. Make sure that you don't damage any roots.

2. Put the root ball into a bucket of water and let it soak for an hour or more. This will help your strawberry plant transition from its temporary pot to the ground and keep the

root system moist.

3. Start digging a hole in the soil. Make sure that the soil has lots of compost or added with enough amendments.

4. Put the strawberry plant into the hole and make sure the crown is above the ground line.

5. As you add soil around the strawberry plant, press the soil gently and firmly around its base.

6. Keep doing the same thing for your other strawberry plants. Make sure that each plant is around 35 to 40 centimeters apart from another. If you are going to plant in rows, make sure that there is a distance of 90 centimeters from each plant.

7. Water your strawberry plants regularly, but don't over water them. The shallow roots of your strawberries need to be hydrated from getting a lot of sunshine all day, but they will grow poorly if their roots are soggy. So make sure that the soil is not too dry but not at all muddy. Do take note that when you water your strawberries, make sure that you will water the crown of the plant and not the fruits since this will cause them to rot.

8. Regularly fertilize your strawberry plants using a water-soluble fertilizer. Use the fertilizer as recommended on its label. Avoid using fertilizers which are high in nitrogen since this will only cause the leaves to grow more and

hamper the growth of fruits.

9. When the strawberry plants start flowering, take off the first flowers. This will allow the strawberry plants to speed up growth and produce stronger roots. When they start to flower again, leave them be and allow them to grow.

10. After a month, you may see some runners growing from your strawberry plant. Take out some of the runners and leave one runner to grow and create new plants. Don't let more than one runner grow since this will deplete the energy of your plant and lessen its chances of producing strawberries.

11. You will discover that strawberries are starting to grow in your plants when you see small green berries, which will turn red when they ripen.

12. You will know that it is time to harvest when the strawberries are entirely red. Pick the strawberries straight from the bush while making sure that the stem is still intact. Wash your strawberries with cold water before eating them.

13. If there are birds or critters going in and out of your garden, consider setting up a barrier around your strawberry plants. You can do this by spreading a strawberry net or fine garden mesh over your plants.

HOW TO PLANT STRAWBERRY SEEDS

Materials:

- Strawberry seeds
- Container
- Soil
- Plastic Wrap

STEPS:

1. You can purchase seeds in garden centers or through mail-order seed companies online. Choose which variety is best for your local climate and environment. Disease-resistant varieties are also highly recommended.

2. Fill your container with soil. Water it thoroughly that it is moist but not muddy.

3. Use your finger to make one-fourth inch holes in the soil, making sure that the holes are six inches apart.

4. Put three seeds in each hole using your fingers or a tweezer.

5. Cover the seeds with a little bit of soil. Don't press your fingers too much in the soil since this might compact it and make the seedlings struggle to grow.

6. Cover the container with a plastic wrap. This will ensure that the soil is moist while the seeds are germinating.

7. Place your container of strawberry seeds in a location that gets adequate sunlight all day. This will help in the

germination process of the strawberry seeds. If you are planting during winter, place your container near a heat source or radiator.

8. Water your seeds regularly. Make sure that the soil is moist but not muddy. Regularly check the soil to make sure that it isn't dry. Your strawberry seeds need a moist soil most of the time.

9. When the strawberry seeds start sprouting, take out the plastic wrap from the container. Regularly check your soil for any dryness and water the seedlings properly.

10. After the strawberry seeds have sprouted, pinch or snip off the smallest plants and leave about six inches between the remaining plants.

HOW TO PROPAGATE STRAWBERRY PLANTS FROM RUNNERS

Steps:

1. If you have a strawberry plant in a container, fill another container with soil. Set this container beside your strawberry plant that is growing some runners.

2. Pick up one of the strawberry plant's runners and push it into the container filled with soil. Leave it attached to the main plant. Cover a portion of the runner with soil, while the other side has to stick out over the other container to maintain its balance. If you are growing strawberries in a

garden bed, simply do the same thing but on an empty space in the ground six inches away from the main plant.

3. Let the runner in this position sit for at least thirty days. Water the main plant and the runner regularly to maintain soil moisture and promote healthy root growth.

4. After thirty days, cut the runner from the main plant using clean garden snips.

FIVE

Growing Berries In Containers

Growing berries in containers is a very resourceful and creative way to grow these superfoods even if you don't have much space to garden. Container gardens can be located anywhere in the house as long as they get adequate sunlight and they are near a water source. They are also relatively low maintenance since your energy and resources are only directed on potted plants, and not an entire garden space.

GROWING BLUEBERRIES IN CONTAINERS

Tips:

1. Choose high bush varieties such as half-highs or dwarfs when you decide to plant blueberries in containers. They grow well in small spaces inside or outside your home.

2. Make sure that your potting soil is acidic enough for the blueberries to thrive well. You can buy potting soil mixes that are specific for acid-loving plants. You can also make your own acidic soil mix by blending one-half part potting soil and one-half peat.

3. Choose a large container to grow your blueberry into. Get something that is at least 2 feet wide and 2 feet deep with drainage holes in the bottom. If you are recycling containers, drill random holes at the bottom. Put a tray underneath the container to catch any excess water.

4. Place your blueberry inside the container in such a way that its roots is just below soil level.

5. Then cover the top of the soil with one to two inches layer of bark mulch.

6. Place your blueberry plant in spot where it can get adequate sunshine, such as near a window, balcony, patio, or terrace.

7. Regularly water your blueberry plant. Just keep the soil moist but not too soggy.

8. Consider planting two blueberry plants so that they can pollinate and set fruits. You can also plant several varieties to extend the harvesting season. Blueberries will generally produce fruit during their first year and produce more fruit in the succeeding years.

GROWING CURRANTS & GOOSEBERRIES IN CONTAINERS

Tips:

1. Choose a container that is at least 2 feet wide and 15 inches deep. Currants and gooseberries grow from small

to medium sized bushes, which make them thrive well in containers.

2. Plant your currant and gooseberry bushes in potting soil rich in compost.

3. Place your plant containers in an outdoor area. Currants and gooseberries can withstand the cold outside and they need the winter chill to set fruit. They also need plenty of sunlight for them to grow and bear fruit.

4. Prune the oldest branches of your bushes every winter season or early spring. Currants and gooseberries usually fruit on branches that are at least two or three years old. They will eventually fruit in the upcoming year after every season of growth.

5. Regularly water your berries. Make the soil moist enough but not too soggy. Watering them often will make the berries plump.

6. Fertilize your berry plants with a water-soluble fertilizer every two to four weeks.

7. They will start bearing green berries at first and then turn into red, black, pink, or white depending on their variety. Green gooseberries, on the other hand, will have yellow stripes and become softer.

HOW TO GROW STRAWBERRIES IN CONTAINERS

Tips:

1. Strawberries will grow well in soil that has a pH of 5.3 to 6.5. Check your potting soil with this ratio.

2. Keep your potting soil rich and healthy by adding a substantial amount of compost to the pot once every month.

3. If you are using a narrow and tall unglazed container as a pot for your strawberry, add one-fourth of peat moss before adding potting soil. This increases the container's moisture retention for your plant.

4. If you choose to plant your strawberry on a hanging container or basket, line it with sphagnum moss and fill it with peaty soil. This helps in moisture retention for the strawberry plant to thrive well. The sphagnum moss will also allow the strawberry plant to grow outward to the sides of the pot, which makes it function like an ornamental.

SIX

Planting Calendar

January – February : Start planting strawberry seeds indoors in containers, pots, tubs, or planters.

March – April : Prepare the garden patch for transplanting new strawberry seedlings. If you have existing strawberry plants, continue fertilizing them.

April – May : Start planting early-bearing strawberry plants in the garden patch. If it is still relatively cold outside, put a cold frame around your plants. Remove the cold frame when it starts to get warm so that they can pollinate. Start planting mid and late-bearing varieties at the near end of April.

Remove first flowers and runners from the strawberry transplants to encourage vigorous growth. If there are birds or critters in the vicinity, install a strawberry net or fine garden mesh.

June – July : Start spreading mulch around your strawberry plants. Regularly water them to keep the soil moist. Do not over water that the soil gets muddy. Check the health of your strawberries. Pull out any unhealthy plants. By this time, you can harvest the produce of early-bearing strawberry plants. You can also start propagating new strawberry plants.

July – August : Continue propagating your plants. Regularly water new and old plants as well. By this time, you can harvest mid to late-bearing strawberry plants.

September – October : Trim off the straggly or old parts of the strawberry plants. Start fertilizing for the winter as well.

Continue harvesting strawberries from your perpetual or ever-bearing varieties.

October – November : Prepare your ever-bearing or perpetual varieties for winter by tidying them up.

December – January : Start weeding around your strawberry plants and remove anything that might be the cause of fungal or mold growth. Cover your strawberry plants with a cold frame in the onslaught of the cold season.

SEVEN

Further Information

ONLINE RESOURCES

Cornell Fruit on Berries – This is a great resource on everything about berries from production, harvest, food safety, marketing, labor, and business management strategies. They also have a column on the latest news about berries in different parts of the United States. Plus, you can get the lowdown on what's happening with the different berry grower organizations across the states. You'll also find tools here such as pest management, berry diagnostic tools, nursery guides, and so much more.

Growing Berries and Grapes in Home Gardens – This is a great free resource by the University of Idaho Cooperative Extension System on growing your own berries and grapes. It will educate you on the principles of growing berries and grapes in any setting. It also features examples and diagrams on how to grow different species of berries.

Mother Earth News On Growing Berries – Mother Earth News features helpful resources on how to grow your own berries at home. You'll find insightful tidbits on how to grow your own blueberries, blackberries, raspberries, currants, and other species of berries. They have a table in which you will know what pH your soil must have to effectively grow specific berries and an article on landscaping with berries.

New York State Berry Growers Association – This is a berry growers association which strengthens the community of berry growers and sponsors research on berry varieties. They can also help you find local farms to find fresh berries. If you are planning to grow your own berry farm, you can stay up to date on the industry with this site. If you already have your own farm, bookmark this site to help you stay competitive in the market.

Ontario Berry Growers Association – This is a provincial organization website which features helpful information on locally grown berries and where to find berry farms. They promote the local berry industry as well as fund research activities. You can also find berry information and sumptuous recipes on the site.

BERRY SEEDS AND PLANTS SUPPLIERS

Burpee – Burpee has a great selection of berries to choose from. You'll be able to choose the right berry for your needs as they help you narrow your search to form, spread, height, uses, and so much more. They also have varieties which are resistant to disease, cold, heat, humidity, and drought – helping you procure the right seeds for your climate and environment.

Plant World Seeds – Plant World Seeds has been one of the leading seed suppliers since 1985. You'll be able to find great varieties of berry seeds here, as well as other types of plants to supplement your indoor or outdoor garden. The site has a very easy search feature and everything is categorized cleanly. They also have some completely helpful garden information for your own perusal.

Strawberry Plants – This is perhaps one of the most comprehensive sites about strawberries. They have extensive information on growing strawberries as well as an online store on strawberry plants and seeds. Deemed as a 'one stop for everything related to strawberry plants and growing strawberries', lovers of strawberries need not look any further.

Rare Seeds – They have a wonderful selection of garden seeds which will make your garden beautiful and productive all year round. With helpful descriptions on the seeds that they are selling, you'll be able to choose the right variety for your needs.

RECOMMENDED BOOKS

Growing Berries: How To Grow and Preserve Berries – This book by James Paris aims to give life to your garden and flavor to your kitchen dishes. This guide will help you grow delicious berries – whether they are blackberries, blueberries, currants, and raspberries. This resource promotes fully organic methods of gardening berries, which creates environmental sustainability and an overall healthy lifestyle. Plus, there are delicious and healthy recipes for jams, jellies, and chutneys in this book.

Growing Organic Berries: Everything You Need To Know To Grow Healthy Berries – This five-star book on Amazon provides you with great tips on soil and equipment preparations, basic information, and best practices on gardening berry plants the organic way. You'll get insider tips on how to prep yourself up for the level of difficulty and geographical requirements that berry plants need. You'll also be equipped with planting, fertilization, and harvesting tips for growing blackberries, blueberries, raspberries, and strawberries.

The Backyard Berry Book: A Hands-On Guide to Growing Berries, Brambles, and Vine Fruit in the Home Garden – You'll find hands-on advice from professional horticulturist, Stella Otto, in this lovely book about berry gardening. You'll find essential information on how to grow blackberries, blueberries, currants, gooseberries, grapes, kiwi fruit, lingonberries, raspberries, rhubarb, and strawberries in this book. With a helpful troubleshooting section and insightful seasonal activity calendar, you're good to go with this comprehensive resource.

The Berry Grower's Companion – A great resource written by Barbara L. Bowling, this book is an essential reference for people who want to grow berries for the pleasure of it or for profit. You will discover how extremely versatile and beneficial berries are in this one-of-a-kind guide. This book is jampacked with great information and tidbits for the berry grower in you.

CONCLUSION

If you are just beginning your journey in gardening or if you are veteran, I hope this book was able to shed some light on growing organic berries. I am confident that the combination of the knowledge and strategies presented in this book along with the determination and drive to succeed; anyone will be able to successfully grow organic berries indoors and outdoors

The next step is to put these strategies into action. It is time for you to test your newly acquired knowledge. Remember that knowledge without action will amount to nothing. It is only when the two are combined that success be achieved. I really want to thank you for reading this book and I sincerely hope that you received value from it.

ABOUT THE AUTHOR

Adam Holmes is a self-proclaimed professional hobbyist who loves learning and mastering new things. Jack of All Trades, Master of a Few, Adam has been inspired by experts in fields ranging from Music, Arts, Business and Medicine to learn new things that will not only benefit his life, but the lives of others.

A software architect by day, Adam spends the majority of his free time learning a new hobby or working on an old one. Although Adam enjoys his day job, he believes that the best part about it is that it affords him the ability spend his free time do what he truly loves, learning new things. If there is a how-to book, YouTube video, or course on learning something, Adam will give it a go, more often than not, mastering the activity within 6 months. The key to success is his unrelenting work ethic, claims Adam. "The majority of people have the capacity to master any skill within 6-9 months if they truly focus all their time and resources on it. It comes down to a will and determination to continue with the activity and see it though. That's where most people fail, not because they aren't physically or mentally equipped."

Adam's newest hobby which he hopes on mastering is writing and self-publishing. Adam plans on releasing several books that give step-by-step guides on how to master a specific activity, marketed towards those who have zero experience in said activity. By sharing so much of the knowledge he has accumulated over the years, Adam hope to help others who want to learn something new by showing them the fast track to mastery.

MORE BY CLYDEBANK

Growing Marijuana For Beginners :

Cannabis Cultivation Indoors & Out

By: Adam Holmes

Visit : http://bit.ly/growcannabis

Companion Planting For Beginners :

Simple Ways To Dramatically Increase

Crop Productivity With Companion Planting

By: Adam Holmes

Visit : http://bit.ly/comp_planting

Preview Of :

Companion Planting for Beginners - Simple Ways To Dramatically Increase Crop Productivity

CHAPTER ONE: Companion Planting Benefits

Better plant growth

Trees or taller plants provide shade or act as a windbreak for other smaller plants that are sensitive to the weather, such as the scorching summer sun or harsh winds. Another historical example of how plants grow better through companion planting is the Three Sisters planting method of the Indigenous Peoples in America. This method involves planting squash, maize, and common beans, which benefit each other well.There are even certain plants that improve their flavor when planted in close proximity to companion plants. There are also companion plants that help provide nitrogen fixation to enrich the soil for other plants.

Increase in agricultural yields

Growing different crops in the same plot of land increases the chances of yielding a better harvest. If plants are grown on different levels on the same land, which may involve planting one as ground cover and another one as trellis, the potential yield of that plot is increased. You'll also ind examples in Chapter III wherein different species thrive more or grow better when planted close to each other.

Pest control

There are various specific examples of how companion plants can protect each other from those horrifying pests or pathogenic fungi. One example is the centuries-old method of Chinese farmers wherein they use mosquito ferns to deter insects from destroying rice crops. Another example is that onions repel pests away from surrounding plants. There are numerous companion plants that are perfect in luring or disrupting pests away as you will soon be reading about in Chapter III.

Attracting creatures which are beneficial to plants

There are certain companion plants that actually attract the predators of pests. Marigolds are known to attract adult hoverflies, and their larvae are the predators of aphids. Some insects are predators of pests in their larvae form, and when they grow as adults they'll eventually become pollinators of plants. It's a win-win situation.

Use Land Efficiently

Gardeners have been using plant combinations, such as vines that grow upward and crops that grow on the ground, to maximize space and produce better yields. Some even grow on various levels that make the most out of the soil's fertility while ensuring that it stays healthy for a long time.

Companion planting is basically a great alternative to modern and mainstream methods of garden maintenance or agricultural farming. It doesn't use artificial fertilizers, pesticides, or weed control. It uses the natural ability of plant combinations for optimum growth and sustainability.

CHAPTER TWO: How To Use This Book

This Book is not just here to inform you about what is and what you can do with companion planting, but to take you by the hand and lead you step-by-step along the way so that you can successfully grow and nurture companion plants in a healthy garden or farm setting.

Step 1: Assess Your Needs

Once you get the gist of companion planting, you'll be tasked to assess your needs in Chapter II as a first step towards establishing the foundation of your companion planting. Whether you are going to start a garden from scratch or already working on an existing garden, the tips and tidbits in Chapter II will assist you in starting or improving your gardening game.

Step 2: Make a Plan

Chapter III allows you to pinpoint the plants from your listed needs in Step 1 (Chapter II) and create a gardening plan to follow. In Chapter III you'll find a companion plants chart, a planting master plan with samples and a template for you to easily input, and an optional journaling guide for you to document the growth and development of your companion plants garden.

Step 3: Getting Your Hands Dirty – It's Planting Time

You'll be provided with a checklist in Chapter III for you to be one step away from researching, purchasing, and acquiring your needed companion plants. Chapter III also has a printable gardening schedule for you to write your daily and weekly tasks to follow. You can post this anywhere in your home wherein you'll be reminded of your daily pursuit towards a better garden. You can even recruit members of your own family or friends for this endeavor. This is also where the importance of journaling comes inwherein you'll be able to document the process of growing your garden.

Step 4: Don't Just Stop Here, Go Further!

It is said that you start dying when you stop learning. Chapter IV directs you to a number of the best resources out there wherein you can expand your knowledge about companion planting and other related topics. You can also find links to online groups or networks where you can find inspiration, knowledge, and communities all for the love of this wonderful gardening craft. - TO CONTINUE READING, GO TO AMAZON.COM

21807450R00041

Made in the USA
San Bernardino, CA
06 June 2015